D1441965

PETS' GUIDES

Squeak's Guide to

Caring for Your Pet Rats or Mice

Isabel Thomas

Chicago, Illinois

WITHDRAWN

© 2015 Heinemann Library,
an imprint of Capstone Global Library, LLC
Chicago, Illinois

All rights reserved. No part of this publication
may be reproduced or transmitted in any form
or by any means, electronic or mechanical,
including photocopying, recording, taping, or any
information storage and retrieval system, without
permission in writing from the publisher.

Edited by James Benefield and Brynn Baker
Designed by Cynthia Akiyoshi
Picture research by Tracy Cummins
Production by Victoria Fitzgerald
Originated by Capstone Global Library Ltd
Printed and bound in China by RR Donnelley Asia

18 17 16 15 14
10 9 8 7 6 5 4 3 2 1

Library of Congress Cataloging-in Publication Data
Thomas, Isabel, 1979- author.
    Squeak's guide to caring for your pet rats or
mice / Isabel Thomas.
            pages cm.—(Pets' guides)
    Summary: "In this book, Squeak the Mouse
reveals how readers should go about choosing
pet rats or mice, what supplies they will need, how
to make a new pet rat or mouse feel at home,
and how to properly care for pet rats or mice,
including feeding, exercising, and keeping cages
clean. Text is accompanied by clear, labeled
photographs to further reinforce key concepts,
and the use of an animal narrator also allows the
book to be used to teach perspective"—Provided
by publisher.
    Includes bibliographical references
and index.

ISBN 978-1-4846-0264-5 (hardcover)
ISBN 978-1-4846-0271-3 (paperback)
ISBN 978-1-4846-0287-4 (eBook PDF)
1. Rats as pets- Juvenile literature
1. Title.
SF459.R3
636.935'2-dc23   2013040458

Acknowledgments
We would like to thank the following for permission
to reproduce photographs: Alamy: © blickwinkel,
21, © Juniors Bildarchiv GmbH, 12, 17, 18, 27;
Capstone Library: Karon Dubke, 10, 23, 25;
Getty Images: Chris Scuffins, 7, Ron Levine, 5,
9; Glow Images: ARCO / Schulte, front cover;
Superstock: Big Cheese Photo, 15; Design Elements
Shutterstock: iBird, Picsfive, R-studio

We would like to thank Eric Jukes for his assistance
in the preparation of this book.

Every effort has been made to contact copyright
holders of material reproduced in this book. Any
omissions will be rectified in subsequent printings
if notice is given to the publisher.

All the Internet addresses (URLs) given in this
book were valid at the time of going to press.
However, due to the dynamic nature of the
Internet, some addresses may have changed,
or sites may have changed or ceased to exist
since publication. While the author and publisher
regret any inconvenience this may cause readers,
no responsibility for any such changes can be
accepted by either the author or the publisher.

Contents

Some words are shown in bold, **like this**. You can find out what they mean by looking in the glossary.

Do You Want Pet Rats or Mice?

Hello! I'm Squeak and this book is all about pets like me. Rats and mice are **rodents**, and we make great pets. It's fun to watch us play and explore. You can teach us to snuggle in your hands, and even sit on your shoulder.

Before getting pet rats or mice, be sure you can look after us properly. We'll need food, water, and a clean place to live. Plus, we need company, safe toys to play with, and **vet** care if we get sick or injured. In return, we'll be your best friends.

Choosing Your Rats or Mice

It's time to meet some more mice and rats. Check out our different **coats** and colors. Rats and mice have similar needs but are slightly different animals. For example, rats are bigger than mice. They need larger homes and more food.

In the wild, rats and mice live in groups. If
possible, I like to have company, especially
when I am asleep. If you would like to keep
a rat or a mouse, think about buying a friend
for me if you can.

Mice or rats are a good choice if you have no other pets. We're afraid of animals such as cats and dogs. Never keep mice with rats or other types of rodents. We need company of our own kind.

Animal shelters, **rescue centers**, **breeders**, and pet stores are the best places to find us. Ask the on-site expert to help you choose mice or rats that know each other. For example, girl mice make good pets, but boy mice may fight each other. Boy mice often have smelly pee, so be careful where you keep them.

Getting Ready

It's time to choose a home for your mice or rats. The bigger, the better! Get a large cage with different levels, things to climb, and places to hide. Don't forget toys and material to build nests and dig burrows.

Squeak's shopping list:

- a large wire cage (for rats) or **aquarium** (for mice)
- hay or shredded paper for building nests
- bedding material deep enough to dig in
- boxes or flower pots for hiding
- tunnels, branches, and ropes for climbing
- a water bottle and food dish
- a special gnawing toy

Welcome Home

Moving to a new home can be scary.
Mice or rats will look for a dark place to hide
until we feel brave enough to start exploring.
Watch us carefully to make sure we don't fight.

Help us to settle in by finding the perfect place for our cage. Choose somewhere away from bright lights, **drafts**, and loud noises. Mice and rats rest and sleep during the day, so make sure we won't be disturbed.

How to Pick Us Up

Early morning and evening are the best times to handle rats and mice. We'll be awake and ready to play. Follow my tips to make sure your pets love being held.

🐾 Wash your hands before and after handling me.

🐾 Talk to me and feed me treats to show you are friendly.

🐾 Gently scoop me up with cupped hands.

🐾 If I poop, pee, or try to escape, it might mean I'm frightened. Put me back and try later.

🐾 Never pick me up by my tail.

🐾 Sit on the floor so I don't get hurt if I jump out of your hands.

Playtime

Mice and rats love exploring. Fill our home with tunnels, ropes, ladders, and ramps for climbing. Get a special rat or mouse exercise wheel. Scatter food around my cage so I can play hide and seek.

When I'm used to being handled, let me play outside my cage. This is my chance to run, jump, and explore a new area. Make sure there are safe hiding places. Keep dangerous things out of reach in case I nibble them.

Feeding Time

Special mouse or rat food contains everything we need to stay healthy. Give us fresh pellets or cubes every morning and evening, so we always have food to eat. Make sure we always have fresh water, too.

Mice or rats like to nibble fresh fruit. Give us a few small pieces so we don't eat too much or too often. Some human foods make delicious treats, but others can make us very ill. Check out my tips on page 29.

Clean and Healthy

Rats and mice are very clean animals. We spend lots of time **grooming** ourselves. Some of us like a bowl of shallow water to dip our faces and paws. Sometimes we fill it with food or bedding though. We're all different!

Like all rodents, I have front teeth that never stop growing. Ask your pet shop for special toys or wooden blocks that your mice or rats can gnaw. This will stop their teeth from growing too long.

Cleaning My Home

I clean myself, but I can't clean my cage. Clear away old food, droppings, and damp bedding every day. Sometimes I pee in one place in my cage, so please clean here a lot! Wash your hands after touching my toys – I pee on things to make them smell like home!

Clean out the whole cage every week. Do it in the morning or evening when I'm already awake. Remember to wash my water bottle and toys. Leave some old nesting material behind so my cage still smells like home.

Visiting the Vet

Most pet mice and rats live for two or three years. Take us to the vet every birthday for a check-up.
The vet will make sure we're happy and healthy. They will check that our teeth are growing properly.

I can't tell you if I'm feeling unwell. Check me every day when we play and when you clean out my cage. Look for anything that is different from normal. Take me to the vet right away if you think I'm sick or injured.

No Change, Please!

Groups of rats or mice like to stay together for life. Please don't split me up from my friends, or put new pets in my cage. We might start fighting. If your rats or mice start fighting, make sure they have enough space, food, toys, and hiding places.

If you go away, please ask someone to visit your house every day to look after us. Tell them how to clean our cage and feed us. They can let us out to play, but be careful they don't lose us! We'll look forward to seeing you again though!

Rat and Mouse Facts

- Rats and mice can hear sounds that you can't hear. They even "speak" to each other using squeaks that are too high-pitched for your ears.

- Big, open spaces make rats and mice feel scared. They always like to be near a safe hiding place.

- Rats and mice love to burrow and build nests. The nests help them to keep warm.

- Rats and mice can squeeze through very small holes. A young mouse can fit through a hole the size of a pencil!

Squeak's Top Tips

Check my water bottle daily to make sure I haven't blocked it with my bedding.

I love eating seeds, grains, and oats. Too many seeds or grains will make us unhealthy. Feed us oats sometimes instead!

Some human foods make great treats, too. Try bread, cooked pasta, and breakfast cereals.

Never give rats and mice grapes, raisins, corn, citrus fruits, onions, chocolate, sticky foods, rhubarb, walnuts, lettuce, or food made for other pets.

Try to avoid traveling with us. If you do, make sure never to leave us in a hot car for a long time.

Glossary

animal shelter organization that cares for animals that do not have homes

aquarium tank with glass or plastic walls used as a home for fish or other small pets

breeder person who helps animals to have babies in an organized way

coat fur or hair that covers an animal

draft cool breeze inside a building from an open door or window

gnaw bite or chew something again and again

groom clean an animal's fur or skin

rescue center organization that rescues animals that are lost, injured, or not being taken care of properly

rodent type of animal with front teeth that never stop growing, like rats and mice

vet person trained to care for sick and injured animals

Find Out More

Books

Birney, Betty G. *Humphrey's World of Pets.*
    New York: Puffin Books, 2013.

Morgan, Sally. *Rats and Mice* (Pets Plus).
    Mankato, Minn.: Smart Apple Media, 2013.

Websites

Learn more about caring for pet mice at:

http://aspca.org/pet-care/small-pet-care/mouse-care

Discover more about rats at:

http://humanesociety.org/animals/rats

Index